Copperhead

Copperhead

poems
Rachel Richardson

Carnegie Mellon University Press
Pittsburgh 2011

Acknowledgments

Grateful acknowledgment is made to the following publications, in which some of these poems first appeared:

32 Poems: "99°" *Blackbird*: "Children Born after the War," "Swamp Ode" *Center: A Journal for the Creative Arts*: "Mississippi" *The Fourth River*: "Nocturne: Benton, Louisiana" *The Hopkins Review*: "Note, upon Learning That Jimmie Davis Did Not Compose 'You Are My Sunshine'" *Hunger Mountain*: "On the Morning of _____'s Execution" *Margie*: "Say Amen" *Memorious*: "Blues" *Michigan Quarterly Review*: "Clearing: 1868," "Relic" *New England Review*: "Cottonmouth" *New South*: "Dan Emmett Writes 'Dixie,' 1859," "Signs" (all "[sign]" fragments) *Ninth Letter*: "Field Notes" *The Pinch*: "Audubon at Oakley Plantation" *PN Review*: "Fable" *Shenandoah*: "Portrait of Leadbelly in Pinstriped Suit" *Slate*: "The Horses" *Southern Cultures*: "Photograph, 1983," "Sandbagging" *Southern Review*: "My Grandmother Plays Emily in Our Town," "Portrait of Britney Spears, Kentwood, 1996" *storySouth*: "Bossier Parish" *Washington Square*: "Natchez Trace, Southbound" *Witness*: "The Refrain"

This book was made possible by support of the Wallace Stegner Fellowship at Stanford University. Special thanks also to the University of Michigan, Dorothy Sargent Rosenberg Memorial Fund, and New Pacific Studio for the gifts of time and space to write. The Squaw Valley Community of Writers and Sewanee Writers' Conference provided valuable camaraderie and critique.

This book could not have been written without the support of my family, Edith Jackson, Kelly Richardson, Lisa Richardson, and especially my father, Thomas Richardson, and my grandmother, Dorothy Richardson. Thanks to my many teachers, especially Cleopatra Mathis, Eavan Boland, Ken Fields, Simone Di Piero, Bill Ferris, Linda Gregerson, and Diann Blakely. For helping me to imagine this book, and for making me work harder, I am grateful to the Black Dog Poets: Lyrae Van Clief-Stefanon, Amy Meckler, Thomas Watson, Andrew Allport, and Rachel Nelson. For fellowship and critical eyes, I am indebted to Jay Pearson, Shara Lessley, Raymond McDaniel, Jeff Hoffman, Karin Goodfellow, Jaswinder Bolina, Sara Houghteling, Rebecca Black, and Ellen Bryant Voigt. I am also grateful to Lola Bell and Permelia Lee for their trust and goodwill. And to David Roderick, my first, last, most generous reader.

Book design: Chelsey Delaney

Library of Congress Control Number 2010928358
ISBN 978-0-88748-536-7

10   9   8   7   6   5   4   3   2   1

for my father

Contents

III

Copperhead:

U.S. *A nickname given, during the Civil War, to a northern sympathizer with the Secessionists of the south.*

—Oxford English Dictionary

The Copperhead, also known in different localities by the names Upland Moccasin, Chunkhead, Deaf Adder, Pilot Snake, etc., is perhaps to be more dreaded than any other American snake.

—Scientific American, *1903*

Nocturne: Benton, Louisiana

There are places in this world telescopic and strange,
the dark like a powerline—a thin grid sings its single note, falling
into my hair, across my back, netting me down
in some wide field. This would be mine: wet razor grass,
moonlight's new country, heat
nestled in leaves.

My father's voice, low, sacred, haunts me
the way wisteria curls into the burnt sharecroppers' cabins,
still here, and wraps the old headboards, floods
across cots. Each word humming, held—

I

Natchez Trace, Southbound

On my windshield, the tiny backs
of insects break. The bleak
gravel heart of the crossroads
lifts its diamond sign, yellow,
its cross a split black eye.

Startled animals gleam
at roadside, each a study in vanishing.

When a squirrel darts
into my path, its eyes too low to warn,
I hear my breath more
than its crush. Barely a noise
to name me for certain.
But I am only passing;
the world keeps its silence.
No one blames me for a thing.

The Refrain

I am learning, with the dark hand guiding mine,
    how to enter the small body of fig, how to scoop the flesh

in one motion, bring it to the bowl, cupped
    from its leather case—garnet, quivering.

I see the folded hand around mine, dry ridges,
    the heavy plain. I feel its press

and loosening, the way into skin, the excavation
    of fruit, egg-seeds and all. And it's this moment

when my grandmother enters—I never remember
    what was said, only the look of her in the doorway,

the eyes I thought for a moment were slit
    even when they were open. I won't recall gestures, or

the way Lola looked, hands in the air above her,
    pulled away from mine, mouth probably closed, no spot

on that white uniform. The figs like fish eyes
    upturned in the bowl. Their peeled skins collapsed and wet.

The city rolls, *Sweetport* on the tongue. Its river a ribbon, its belly cinched tight.

Sometimes I see my grandmother again, young, lifting a linen shirt over her head. All around her, morning glory breathes. Everything wants to touch that skin.

Sign: The United Nations wants to take away your GUN

These are the materials.
These are the materials—

Snakebit

Snakebit was my favorite game—
I'd play the girl, the maiden, pinned
under tucked sheets

on the fold-out. My sister's breath
steadied so I knew she was asleep. Only
then, eyes squeezed, could I begin

to assemble the snake. It shifted,
patterned, until I believed it
real: sand-brown, a cold

symmetry spurring its tight length.
Conjured, it raised its head—
always in my grandmother's house;

nights, the fan whirred.
At opposite ends of the hall
the elders slept. I shut my eyes—

the river's edge sparked
and the snake came. I writhed.
My sister rolled, sometimes

sighed—the serpent froze
midstrike. When all was clear,
I strolled the levee

pretending not to see.
I could *feel* the coil,
the poison coursing

upward. I looked
the snake in both eyes—a million
needles, a million blinding

knives. *Snakebit.* I loved
saying it, as I rocked
on my hands, *snakebit*

as tiny creaks leaked from
the fold-out bed. The air's slow
stirring releasing inch by inch

the night. The girl
of my dreams not yet dead,
but *snakebit*, her body

tasting the poison, rising:
the pinned girl inventing the snake,
inventing the venom.

Portrait of Britney Spears, Kentwood, 1996

From the first it was Let's pretend
           and the game had a beat behind it,
      sinewy and breathing. She belted praises

in the Baptist choir. The Latin boys
           at the Quick Stop watched her walk,
      and her math teacher leaned close

to her desk, examining her proof.
           She smelled like watermelons, blushed
      when they voted her prettiest in school.

And Britney in the bathroom: oh the girls
           crowded her even while she glossed
      her lips. The agent told her mother

she'd be a symbol of the New South,
           and took her to a dogtrot house
      for the shoot. She'd brought her own

pink halter, whose ties she knew
           brushed her bare skin when she moved.
      She understood his vision right away:

she should grasp the whitewashed
           column like a pole,
      hold it like she'd never left

her home. He said Just pretend
　　　　you're a prisoner, or a slave, yes, yes,
and keep your eyes right here.

The Scale

The swamps and the silver coffee tray I loved with equal passion. And, too, finding a robin's nest flung to the ground in wind, with three of its eggs destroyed, and three babies bleating.

The world was nothing if not fair. Bread almost broke itself into halves.

And my father courted the night, roaming block by block as if to divide the city were to understand. Under streetlights, orbs of pollen fell onto asphalt, onto cars.

"What's the difference between a live _____ and a dead _____?" a friend of my grandmother's asked, elbow to my ribs, a secret grin poisoning his face. He had me alone in the sitting room, among Chinese silk cushions.

A place for silence and a place for speech. Fried chicken is an induction. Beer cans on the stoop.

One evening at the Hobbit Shop, green in the night-lit emptiness, she threw a party to introduce us to the neighborhood girls. A stuffed lion moodily shadowed a train on a circular track. The arms of porcelain dolls reached for finger sandwiches on trays.

In the grass, I could sometimes hear the insects as they worked. Come in, come in, my grandmother or Lola would say from the door. What are you doing sitting in your nice church clothes in the yard?

This was the year of the tornado, where afterwards I was allowed to keep the robins in a box, sheltering them with string and dry needles gathered from the broken pines.

It's true I pressed my face to the conditioned air vents in the Buick. Also that one day, in anger, my sister threw me into the Robinsons' pool.

Because to divide is God's will?

Underwater, I tried to pretend I had jumped on purpose, crossing my legs in my billowing rose-print dress. I raised an imaginary teacup to my lips, determined to remain until someone fished me out.

———————————

(sweet tea / big girl / get up off your knees)

The lesson is: stop crying. Flies are drawn to honey, not vinegar. This is how a girl gets what she wants. Beaucoups dollars, shoes.

Sometimes a bridge goes over a river. Sometimes it goes over a road.

Sign: Bible answers will be given to many Q's

———————————

Children Born after the War

Somewhere on the road is everything you want:
cantaloupe, okra, roast peanuts overflowing
their bags. Muscadine jelly and moonshine
syrup, each in a heavy glass jar.
Everything rises: mayhaw choked by cane.

Thank your rubber tires and the smooth coins
in your palm. Thank your grandfather
and his battalions of boys. The road here
to Tulsa is lined with track. And each bright
fruit you tongue out of its shell
comes as if on air—no trace of origin, no thorn.

Relic

The first time I touched it,
cloth fell under my fingers,
the frail white folds
softened, demure. No burn,

no combustion at the touch of skin.
It sat, silent, like any other contents
of any other box: photographs
of the dead, heirloom jewels.

Exposed to thin windowlight it is
exactly as in movies:
a long gown, and where a chest
must have breathed, a red cross

crossed over. The crown, I know,
waits underneath, the hood with eyes
carefully stitched open, arch cap
like a bishop's, surging to its point.

Clearing: 1868

Because in this new world they could not accept
families huddled on their roofs, livestock swept
into silt, cane and cotton pulped, men fashioned
propellers: they would tame the river, break

the sandbars for boats. Delta surveys proved
the utility of this endeavor; Humphreys
rolled the clay bed on his tongue. They stood
at the break, where jungle bows to current, where vine

and willow defer; they "watched the dark boiling
of the beast itself." Their ship they christened
Essayons, their girl of curling blades.
She would fight the channel upstream to its shallows

and dredge the bars to bits. "This river shall no more
taunt us," they said, "with its obsidian lips."

Portrait of Leadbelly in Pinstriped Suit

In the distance, wild blue cane, the fugitive strain.

He bows   *in them old cotton fields back home.*

Angola: twelve-bar blues, fiber thick in his fist

and the law cuts him deals, leads him in and out of farms.

The boll is parenthesis, the weevil his voice.

And the city takes him back, in soot-stained arms,

furnace breath, to joints he shakes like the devil

has shimmied up inside his leather boot.

Blue cane in ten-foot topsoil, where no man dares plough.

Because one day he'll raise his head against the whip,

smile at the overseer, swear his name's

Mister Ledbetter, chains or no.   *How sweet the sound.*

by and by / the Junebaby with the sad eyes

Sign: What part of "Thou Shalt Not" don't you understand?

When I was thirteen, fighting, I told my grandmother I had a black boyfriend. I shaped him until he fit my purpose. My early want for weapons.

Mississippi Juvenile Rehab Facility. Trucks pulling their horses. Bogue Chitto River. Elvis at the Hayride. It's called the War of Northern Aggression. Lake Dixie Springs, near McComb.

More instrumentals.

Blues

Even the black is blue.
Even the cargo ship, a shrimp or lobster
boat or bigger, black-blue

against the fog and cerulean water.
And the boys and girls running in the water:
bruise-glowed, five-fingered outlines paused

like bent stars, kicking at the icy
froth of water, crouching for a blue-striped
beachball. It's that line in the back,

above the water and below the fog
that draws my eye—only because
the rest of the picture is so blue does this low air

appear white. A hollow-lostness white,
a pull to something distant, let's say.
Truly it is blue, as wet and deep-evening

as the ocean, the sand, the steamer, the beachball,
or the boys or the girls or the shine of the picture
glossing all their faces to blue.

Only my want for contrast invents it white—
as when given so much of one good thing
my eye searches for the lack.

Deed

All along the Atchafalaya,
all along the Red, men are making deals,
signing papers to trade their land
for promises of help after the flood.
Every good citizen destroys his crop
to save the city below.

But my great-grandfather,
long in the legacy of staunch Stinson men,
meets the state man at the levee
with a shotgun of his own. Refusing
to stand down, he hoists the barrel above his head
and swears to the churning skies
he will not move, not sign—
only water can drag him from this height.

    • • •

No: it is lost already.
It is weeks later; he sits in the portrait studio
with a stern-faced wife and the baby girl in white
on her knee. His cornfield is a swollen lake.

When night came to the levee,
the state man gone, every farm
north and south buckling to the flood,
he knew the battle lost. He stood in the dark,

and then walked back down.

In the picture he is inscrutable;

a crack in the sepia runs the length of his face.

Sandbagging

Louisiana State Penitentiary, Angola, 1997

To highway-road,
    to rock-build.
To tree-split,
    fence-string,
hammer.

Prisoner porter,
    prisoner freight.

To hammer,
    to hammer.

You hold bags open,
    you funnel
the sand.
    You tie them
closed and load
    here,
to the truckbed.

Prisoner faithful,
    prison of storms.

To harbor
        and winnow,
to salvage.
        Your mothers
unmothered,
        you bolster.

The warden says fill
        and you fill it.

The river says
        break
                and you still it.

Note, upon Learning That Jimmie Davis
Did Not Compose "You Are My Sunshine"

Jimmie Davis, I needed you
walking the earth the Singing Governor,
who rode his horse up the capitol steps.

You, pacing those marble rooms with her warmth
still wafting around you, as you turned on your heel
to override the city politicians

whining in your ear. *Snakes in the grass, every one,*
my father said. You were our star,
cowboy boots stamping the Senate floor.

How many times did I imagine your journey,
farmhouse to the wide stone steps,
on the sloping back of Sunshine—

and your dismount, celebrated by hordes
of photographers each morning. And then
how you turned in toward her neck,

stroked the mane, and began to sing?
Could you really have bought the words
from some poor boy, years before, who had

scribbled and hawked them, with dozens more,
in the state university quad as *the perfect elixir
for love?* I heard the way your voice rose

in the opening notes, how you lingered
on her name—I believed this was something
you made for her. But perhaps

you only rode her as a beast. You made her
what she became: barrier to the building,
muscled flanks enforcing your stance

against integrating schools. Did my father know this?
When he told me you *strode*—and with such pride
as if they were his own long steps—

did he know the horse was only a horse,
and you spat on the ground
to make your point? Did he know

I wanted to be her, someone's Sunshine?
I wanted to follow and he delivered you, crooning.
For years no one lured me away.

II

Field Notes

My grandmother is not hurting anyone. Blackberry and dewberry vines will cover all this in a month or two. King's Jambalaya Café and the Lucky Lady Lounge.

Thursday, I wrote. *Call Grand Hotel Avoyelles. AAA.*

My grandmother's gas checks come the first of the month. When you catch a snapping turtle, you have to cut the line. A book of climbers and trailers, and the magnolias just beg. *1 SE to Marksville*, I wrote.

There is this, and then there is the other thing.

Bees hiving. When you catch a snapping turtle, let it have the bait. Leadbelly sang himself off the prison farm, and look where it got him.

Here: satin, towtruck, juke joint. Bourbon, broken tree limb, iodized salt.

She says no one's lived in this cabin twenty years. The roof was falling even then.

New supermax brings jobs up the road in Evangeline Parish. New Walmart brings jobs two miles down. *People want a better quality of life*—and there is this, the other thing.

The television's tuned to storms. Stopped and looked out because I thought I saw light, *but again,* I wrote, *there is none.*

Sweet tea at the Shreveport Club. Crepe myrtle, hidden river. Barbed wire means no trespass. Who wants to see the menace every day?

Armadillo, armored, stiff, at roadside. Someone asked if I wore armor when I went into the prison. I said I only brought poems.

Vine's holdfasts slither beneath strips of bark, says the book on shrubs and vines.

Mrs. Nicholson has hired a guide to lead tours of her haunted house. My grandmother rocks in her chair, not hurting anyone. I am driving the levee. Cut it all loose for a turtle. Count yourself lucky with loss.

31N to Lake Martin Road. *Terrace Inn 517-253-5274.* A woman traveling alone—this, and the other thing. Confederate ghost, electric chair, antiques: people have to earn their keep.

Vines will cover all this in a month or two.

My grandmother, not hurting, my tracks on the road.

Another flood warps the tongue-and-groove floor-
boards and the Lucky Lady Lounge. Walmart brings jobs
two miles down.

49N to Alexandria, then home, I wrote.

The tour guide is the only one who believes in the ghost.

Fable

No one's heard of the man I've invented
to marry, from another parish and all dressed in rags,
no hat on his head and no coat, either.
No one's heard his walking step, the way his boots
drag against the dirt like steel balls, like his feet
are his binding, like he's coming for me
against his own bound body. And his body
in rags, my marrying man, his body in rags and his head
clean of hair. No one's heard of this man or his name
or his family, no one knows his next of kin if he dies.
No one thought to ask at the store who he looked for
or could they help him, my silent man
with his heavy-lid eyes. No one's heard of him, so
how will he find me, how will he come down our small street
and call for me by name, if he can't find my name
because there's no one to help him, and the postmistress
doesn't give addresses to strangers—how will he
come for me in my father's house, and bang
on the door, and find me, my body in rags, no coat, my skin
wasting? How will he wake me from my dream
in which he woke me and took my hand
and walked me past the church and the theater,
and told me *Say goodbye to all this* and I did?

A Hanging: February 1, 1929

Crime passionelle, they said:

                    Ada, a woman
like myself, but no—contract killing, they
    called it.   Two lovers enter
    a sharecropper's cabin in another town, but
        close enough to be known—
and would be discovered, the heat and fleas,
    the *darkness*,   some would say,
of such an act—
and he a doctor no less, who had delivered
    her children,   and she with a good
        husband hand-in-hand with her to church.

A *woman!* they said: she planned it
    herself.
And once they decided to make her
an example   she must have known her fate—
    the governor could bet his career
on a case like this.

The intricacy   of the plot, how
they loved it, every word
        assuring her guilt.   She wrote a letter
to the doctor: her husband would take her
to the lake, their pirogue
    navigating past cypress stumps and she
lure him   into the open night.

If such a one is to live, the prosecutor
told the jury (not a single
     Cajun among them, which pleased him
no end) and let his sentence
        trail.

She would be the first
white woman the state took
       by the neck—
and, knowing it, she shut her mouth.   Stared them down.

    A woman like myself.
The transcript records only her request
for the rope.

In a different life he might have been my lover. In this life he couldn't keep. I saw no difference, love from owning.

(bands of light / heat lightning / heat blisters / some ancient city)

KFC: "We Now Have Gizzards"

Make music of anything you have.

Cottonmouth

swung low, o elliptical
pilot, your hidden eye—

ache for everything, strict
narrative, o cotton

long sleeping, mouth open
trapjaw, spilled black

through water—warm
searchlight, eat moving

o pilot green water
your angular face—

ache open, bear young
live and blinking

—dear skimmer, dear compass
hollow belly and stout

bend your length low—
o chariot, raw cotton

spit crossband and slide,
guard entry—coil skin

and seam skin, dear
water-swallowed pilot

    sweet castoff, most native
—o hunter

    my hanging, o named son
gone wrong—

Dan Emmett Writes "Dixie," 1859

He started with the tune his mother had hummed
in Ohio, nostalgia he'd carried for years,
and by Sunday afternoon he had the words.
A triumph, already; he whistled the banjo's part.

(Himself a sympathizer from the North,
called *copperhead*, called traitor by his own kin.)

Something lively, some *git-up-and-git* they'd wanted
and didn't he deliver—
Miss Susan got seven encores the first night.
That gave them their tune, their Negro walk-around—

Look away, look away, look away, they sang.
Vipers, that spring, spread thick on the ground.

III

I had seen it when coming up-stream,
but I had never faced about to see how it looked
when it was behind me.

—*Mark Twain,* Life on the Mississippi

The Odds

for Jay

I am trying to write a song for you

—you a quiet child from the beginning
decades before I knew you

here is a song
for your coming-to
at the age of sixteen under a wire fence

where your first girl left you,
screaming *If I can't have you no one can*

    • • •

It was a small farm
and not yours and you woke there

a spell binding your limbs,
your muddy hair pressed to your neck

I'm trying to write you a song
because she said

Ain't nothing good coming to you now

and you knew what that meant

You felt your twisted body,
porous as a sieve, the sun breaking in

no memory of how you arrived

and you came-to
looking over at the yard, the hogs looking back
with their unconcerned eyes

    •   •   •

You never believed in voodoo
for a second—the chanting

between us was only our hands, no work
by the dead, only our hands moving
across the darkness

    •   •   •

I gave you once
a picture of a water wheel

because I wanted to show you
the way the water moved

on the wheel,
circled and left and returned

like a nest of snakes,
the bodies married to the turning

I wanted to give you this
picture, this place
your birthright

But I was no voodoo queen
I worked only in this world

   • • •

I was your secret girl
descended from silks

My father fell asleep to the notes of *Dixie*
as a child, swore he could hear

the stars falling on Shreveport
as in all the mourning South

   • • •

You sat on my bed one afternoon
while I opened my first letter from Lola's sister

telling how Lola coddled my father
and waxed the floors with Shinola

I was trying to cross a line

trying to learn something
beyond what I'd been told

You said *No, no, she didn't write this*
look at the handwriting

She had someone
write it for her, maybe her son

      • • •

And now you are driving home
to your own mother in the hospital

doctors don't know what's wrong

so they've sent for you
unhexed and educated

all the way from the North
to tend her

Of course, you say, tired of this line

When do doctors
ever know what's wrong

with a poor black woman?

. . .

You were a quiet child from the beginning
born by mistake

in the factory where your mother worked
packaging chickens, a knowing child

you were told hush right away
and you listened

at least I imagine you did

I didn't know you then, a baby with milken eyes
taking in the sparking machines,
the wires, the partitions

each man to his labor
the assembly line   you were taking in

the rotating blade to slice the neck, the breasts,
like a water wheel, like what Ezekiel saw

a wheel inside a wheel

a call within a call

• • •

I would not meet you for thirty years
I could not meet you

I wasn't born I couldn't travel
How could I know what to look for?

I'd have to study my magic
I'd have to put a spell on that girl

then pull on my boots and tromp my way
through the hanging vines

skirt the gators   squash the snakes

suck their poison out of my own leg
cover six parishes

meet the neighbors, camp under
the willows   I'd have to

get permission from the judge
or defy his order

where there was no route, make one

If I ever slept, I would lose the way

99°

Mustn't there be a hole—
somewhere, in all
this heat?
      A mouth
of rain that unhinges
its jaw?
      Untamps
the frog's defeated
tongue?
      Bids the dog rise
from his belly in dirt?

Someone, open
the chambers.
      Walls
lurch against their own
doors.
      The trestle
moans *under, under*
with the train.

Let the minute hand
unfasten itself.
      Jars
not covet the ground.
Beget the jellies
      back into juice.
At least
let the livestock sleep.

A letter to Jay in my head, one I won't write: *I never used you like a gun. But if I cannot say I loved you, if I hold all this noise inside. . . .*

(Line Avenue / briars)

Sign: GOD BLES SAMERICA

Lullaby among Oil Fields

A great machine
drilling a hole in the earth
is only a lover
stroking the sleeping
beloved, and the land
rolls over, docile,
nothing wailing
or cracking apart—
it just shimmers
and refolds.

We were children,
very young,
born of this black-gold.

My Grandmother Plays Emily in *Our Town*

I

I am asking something gone
return: at least one night, her face

a girl's, just twenty, and
to be married in a month,

holding the dress's hem to her lips
as places are called. And I,

come along too late to know her
trembling, parting the curtain—

let me hear her now
perched on the ladder, recite

"But Mama, . . .
am I pretty enough . . . ?"

II

When Emily marries, ladies in hats
drown out the proper vows

—it's what the play requires:
the everyday over the sacred. Even the set

is made of items found in the actors' garages
so we always see back to the bones.

Here my grandmother stands at the altar
with her fictional George

and gossip swells in the pews
which are rows of folding chairs.

III

Among the murmuring departed,
in the cemetery,

my grandmother takes
her place at the empty plot.

She's the newcomer
who can't believe she's dead

if the living roam
just on the crest of this hill.

My grandmother in white
poplin dress and hair ribbon

lifts her arms in despair—
Emily, untouched by the rain.

IV

Tomorrow her face will glow
on the cover of *The Shreveport Times*—

a gorgeous girl demanding her life.
"But oh!" she cries in Emily's voice,

"I can go back there
and live all those days over again. . . ."

V

So Emily steps back
into childhood

though the wiser dead
have told her don't—

into her mother's kitchen,
her twelfth birthday, a moment

she thought she was happy.
She watches now

that life: mother speaking
gruffly, father late to work.

Dead Emily kisses the cheek
of the classmate playing her mother—

understanding, in that kitchen,
they'd all been blind:

they never knew those people
they said they loved.

VI

My grandmother maintains
her grace to the end.

She is the queen of the theater;
all of Shreveport melts for her smile.

She holds her palm out
to feel the heavy drops as the curtains close,

though she knows this rain
is only the sound of rain.

Bossier Parish

Can anyone tell me
what happened to the cracks on the sidewalk
from the air conditioner's drip

or the air conditioner itself,
Mr. Thompson stooping to turn it on
every evening at 5:15

whose cursing I heard
all the way from the street?

Where are the women
leaning on the building for cool,

the beautiful shoulders of the youngest,
the brass of her laugh

and the neon sign for *Coffee Bait & Beer*—

the Buick rolling up the road,
its silver wheels

the man with one leg
shorter than the other

the stack of gas bills
the orange hat Gerald wore
the oak's side crusted with sap?

There is no ledger
for the groans from the house on the corner

and the way they sidled out to the porch after
with one glass of sweet tea between them—

the stack of water bills

the warped card table Mrs. Gallagher left out
in case people came to call

the wooden chair

a scratching under the house

the box of ornaments
under the eaves

the antique piano Lena played, humming
Is you is or is you ain't
my baby?

They are like clouds passing over—

some mornings I wake emptied

longing for her shoulders,
the wounded oak still.

Audubon at Oakley Plantation

I need them true to life
and so I shoot them,
as many as fill the field at dawn,
and then fix wires
to prop them as if feeding their young
or bending to the river.

Why make a little book
when they exist life-sized,
can be etched to stand high as my hip?
Often have I wished
I had eight pairs of hands to hold them,
and another body for the gun.

_____

Two thousand miles between me and Jay. No one spits on
us in the parking lot. No one stops spitting either.

There must be another way to say this.   (instrumentals /
find instrumentals)

Sign: Planter's Bank & Trust

I pass a Mack truck with a lit golden cross on its grill.

I know one thing that kills the pines is red heart decay,
working into the core, bleeding them out for months.

_____

Zydeco at Mulate's

I am wearing a man's hat
slipped over my head
    (where y'all from, y'all?)
toe heel toe

—the local joke: they're all Yankees
north of I-10

so we must be a footnote, that distant, just a dream
someone dreamed.

Blackened catfish, a girl
with a notebook
    (what you want,   what)

my sister two-stepping with a big man
like she knows what she's doing.

Was it a rainstorm
coming in, an electrified night

    howling behind our rented car. . . .

We might be someone's dream
someone's question
    (what you want?)—

I'll bear the hat lower
its brim a crescent over my eyes

    follow the steps:

nothing will stay
but perhaps

Swamp Ode

they take you in
swallow   hipbones   skin
melted   mercy
a fishing boat split by lightning

     they take you in
drift   slip
across the scales of alligators
     slick turtle back   new nubs
of cypress upthrust
for air
     they take you in
     money and all

coiled net of algae   spinning wake

     the clothes off your back
     your sputtering
         lungs

inside
     green   humming

inside
sky   thick silt churns

inside are

inside
    the signatures
of all the saints   crops drowned

children   men

    bending through

Evangeline, to Gabriel

This is the forest primeval —*Longfellow*

I

I've followed the compass-flower,
I've sung your compass-song:

loup garou, loup garou

—I believe the snake
beds down with the swallow,

and the terrible flock (*pelicans*,
like no creature we have known),

might call my name and lead me
—for these great birds

hunt open-mouthed,
their throats enormous gullies.

I too wish to be emptied,
my body built around a hollow.

The river's dried to spit
but I walk it, mud-skinned,

warbling from my feral throat—

loup garou, loup garou

II

One hundred years, and always
you are just ahead—

loup garou, loup garou

—I walk in water's shadow,
take for my bed the deadfall leaves,

build cramped and feeble fires,
now the preacher's gone.

—All I dream is the nest
and the serpent

as if she sang to the swallows,
she promised

each animal selfsame in its skin

—she scaled the distance between them
and when she tired

she hung her body
among the weeping moss—

And yet it is not a question
of what she believes.

The viper, by her nature,
must overtake the nest

and clasp the bird upon striking,
let its poisoned heart vibrate in her throat—

which is why I restrain my hands
each time, in my sleep, you pass.

Mississippi

I'm going to tell it like this:

the river's brushed
    silk, its boats cradled, cattle calm on
    banks, synchronicity
        of water wheels. I'm a child and

you're one too, and
    cotton fields are opening before
    us. This wailing unwailed,
        a photographic trick—sorrow's

no museum.
    Unhinged bones rest safe inside coffins.
    On the banks, rattling cane,
        a cropduster's dive, the small-town

statued saint.
    A pilot corrects the error in
    a compass, they say; I'll
        trace the river backward, to where

antiqued portraits
    pose families on roofs. They're lovely,
    since they're gone. No river
        on fire, no gas lines snapped—none of it

today, unreach-
    able for weeks. This is what I should
    have said before: towns built
        on mud, we love you. Bring back

the drought year blues,
    old Pontchartrain bridge. Cover the dead
    with lace. Here's a story
        to send us off to sleep: *Let's say*

the levees held,
    we entered the old house again. . . .

Say Amen

For Avon skin-so-soft and the
Liberty Baptist Church,
the Family Dollar discount
grocery, this thunderstorm,
heady and thick, the cogs
and the wheels and the sign,
Goats for sale.
For bugs flat to the windshield,
for the Trailwinds bus, the driver
who calls you girl,
his slow syllables, the gum
that rolls over his speaking tongue.
Praise the envelope of night
licked shut, the grasshopper
crawling your neighbor's seat,
his open-mouthed snore, his
smiling eyes, the dream
he's having, the gators
in their swamps . . .

A world of Waffle House and Speedway. Praise every last
rigged hand.

white women have no blues / instead we buy shoes

a little song, more prisons
a new verse, more prisons
passing like the rows of crops

more prisons, a little song

Sign: We Crack Pecans Large and Small

Photograph, 1983

for Lola Bell

When you and my grandmother both got old,
and she could not bear
the empty house, and all your children
were gone as well, some nights the two of you

crawled into her brass bed
"like a pair of old spinsters," your sister
says. I am learning so late
how it was. You and my grandmother:

born the same year, and both
your husbands went to fight in the war,
though yours never returned.
And in this picture—

my grandmother must have taken it—
you're smiling, probably because
we've been told to. And I'm smiling, too,
fierce with new teeth:

we're a girl in an Easter dress
caked with mud, gripped by a woman
half blind, lock-kneed, starched.
We are still standing there, looking out.

The Horses

Under the live oak, and out along the stretch
where the moon lights the gravel white—
they're blinking, flanks brilliant,
they're turning their heads. See them

not going anywhere particular, just standing now
outside the gate because the gate is open again
and the road what's beyond.
Some tilt their snouts up to the branches

to nibble at clusters of mistletoe; one shakes
her mane, loosing flies. Someone left the gate open
so they've walked from the dewy field;
see them gathered, scattered all over the road

under the stars, directionless, blowing warm air
from their nostrils. They have no debt to anyone.
Who knows how long they've stood
there, askew in the night, shuffling

and huffing steam. By morning a man will find them
under the low trees by the river
or in flower beds near town. Not because
they are parched or starving. They walk

because night stretches out, and there is a road,
and someone has opened the gate.

On the Morning of _____'s Execution

Could there be one minute more of singing
anywhere over the whole dry earth this morning? Angola is
    a giant

mousetrap, inescapable, the warden says, with four clamps
in the four directions: *Something always gets 'em.*

Heatstroke, gator, snakebite, a bullet.
                The best thing I know to ask for

is one minute, and what would that do?
When Jay held me in his dark room with the door closed

one minute more, what did it accomplish? Who was less
    wounded
because our bodies met? Still, all the protests

beg that stay. Only stay.
             There was a night

in another country when a woman called to the man
who could not be her husband and brought him to her bed.

She was already beginning to show.
She would drown herself in the well come dawn.

But that night—her lips like a small bowl, her manner polite
till the last—that night she brushed her swollen fingers

from the high bone of his foot up the legs;
she wrote a log of the body through the vessel

of the body.
           I am inventing what happened in her bed

out of a protester's need for rupture: that to add
one minute might change the larger course

of time. Might lead that man even now being strapped
in those crossed leather straps to the chair,

even now being readied to clasp his body to its planes
in the final heaves—in some fifth direction

out of the jungle, off the prison grounds named
for another country. This trap might be our mistake:

someone's belief in the narrow options
of a compass. In heatstroke. And what beyond

the last degree?
           Another minute.

A story is not the way to end a story
that tries to unstrap a man from a chair. A story leaves him

listening, bound. But all I can offer is what I imagine
of that low bed, where the woman had mashed

honeysuckle into the sheets. Where she led her love
by his solid hand. He who would never tell.

Or,
if you'd rather, I'll end with the story I myself

lay down to, with my own lover, night after night,
not because I believed in its narrative

but because everyone outside wanted to kill something,
and if I stayed in here—if I stayed with you, Jay—

perhaps I would not.

Notes

The copperhead (*agkistrodon contortrix*) belongs to the pit viper family, which also includes the cottonmouth and rattlesnake. Frequently known as pilot snakes or moccasins, pit vipers are common throughout the Southern United States.

"[sign]" (p. 17): I have borrowed the phrase "these are the materials" from Adrienne Rich's *An Atlas of the Difficult World*.

"Clearing: 1868": The U.S. Army Corps of Engineers in 1868 built a dredge to try to break apart the sandbars north of New Orleans and clear the Mississippi River for passage. They called it *Essayons* ("we shall try"), having great hopes for the project, but only succeeding in breaking propeller blades. I am indebted to John M. Barry's *Rising Tide* for this and much other detailed information on river control and the flood of 1927.

"Portrait of Leadbelly in Pinstriped Suit": The italicized lines are drawn from Leadbelly's song "Cotton Fields" and the traditional spiritual "Amazing Grace."

"Sandbagging": In 1997, the Mississippi flooded and threatened Louisiana State Penitentiary, Angola. Prisoners were sent to bolster the levees and, after many hours, were able to contain the river and preserve the institution.

"A Hanging: February 1, 1929": On this date, Ada Bonner LeBoeuf became the first white woman to be executed in the state of Louisiana. She and her lover, Thomas E. Dreher, were sentenced to hang for the murder of her husband. Their sentence was delayed for many months until Governor Huey Long refused their final appeal. *The New York Times* covered the trial in the final days, so controversial was the ruling.

"The Odds": The italicized lines "a wheel within a wheel / a call within a call" are from Gillian Welch's song, "I Dream a Highway."

"Audubon at Oakley Plantation": I have paraphrased and recombined selected phrases from Audubon's collected writings.

"Zydeco at Mulate's": This poem is for Kelly J. Richardson.

"Evangeline, to Gabriel": The epigraph for the poem, as well as its premise, are taken from Henry Wadsworth Longfellow's epic, *Evangeline*. Longfellow's poem follows the story of two young Acadian lovers who are separated during the Acadian removal to French Louisiana. They spend many years mournfully searching through the bayous and fields, trying to reunite, always just missing each other.

"Photograph, 1983": I am grateful to Permelia Lee for the line I quote in the poem, as well as for her many other stories that inform this book.

"On the Morning of _____'s Execution": The italicized passage paraphrases Angola's warden, Burl Cain.